★★
★ The Library of
American Landmarks™

THE GOLDEN GATE BRIDGE

Thomas S. Owens

The Rosen Publishing Group's
PowerKids Press™
New York

Published in 1997 by The Rosen Publishing Group, Inc.
29 East 21st Street, New York, NY 10010

First Edition

Book Design: Danielle Primiceri

Photo Credits: Cover © Hilary Wilkes/International Stock; p. 4 Christian Michaels/FPG International; p. 7 © Lambert/Archive Photos; p. 8 © AP/Wide World Photos; pp. 11, 20 © Chuck Szymanski/International Stock; p. 13 © L. D. Smithey/FPG International; p. 15 © Archive Photos; p. 17 © Paul Thompson; p. 19 © Bill Losh/FPG International.

Owens, Tom, 1960–
    The Golden Gate Bridge / Thomas S. Owens.
        p.   cm. — (The Library of American landmarks)
    Includes index.
    Summary: Discusses the history, design, and significance of this architectural wonder.
    ISBN 0-8239-5016-6
    1. Golden Gate Bridge (San Francisco, Calif.)—Juvenile literature. [1. Golden Gate Bridge (San Francisco, Calif.) 2. Bridges.] I. Title. II. Series.
    TG25.S225O84 1997
    624'.5'0979461—dc21   97-11547
                                                                                          CIP
                                                                                          AC

Manufactured in the United States of America

Table of Contents

Bridging the Golden Gate

Until 1937, few people believed that it was possible to build a bridge across California's Golden Gate **Strait** (STRAYT). Some people thought that the water was too deep or that the wind was too strong. Others were afraid that an earthquake would knock the bridge down. Still others thought it would cost too much. But James Wilkins and Joseph Strauss knew they could build a strong, solid bridge.

◄ Until the Golden Gate Bridge was built, people had to cross the Golden Gate Strait by ferry.

Crossing the Bay

The Golden Gate Strait connects the Pacific Ocean to the San Francisco Bay.

Until the early 1900s, ferry boats took people across San Francisco Bay. But the bay can be rough and windy, especially during the winter. The bay can also be foggy and dangerous to cross. In 1916, an **engineer** (en-jin-EER) named James Wilkins wrote a newspaper article suggesting that a **suspension** (sus-PEN-shun) bridge be built across the Golden Gate Strait. Many people thought that was a great idea.

Engineer James Wilkins believed that it would be safer to cross the bay by bridge than by ferry ▶

THE GOLDEN GATE BRIDGE

WASHINGTON

MONTANA

OREGON

IDAHO

WYOMING

NEVADA

UTAH

COLORADO

CALIFORNIA

ARIZONA

NEW MEXICO

The Bridge Builder

Joseph Strauss was a bridge builder. He had built more than 400 bridges in countries all over the world. He was very excited about the idea of building the Golden Gate Bridge. He created a **design** (dee-ZYN) in 1921. By 1933, the bridge and the design were approved. Strauss and many others worked hard to raise the 27 million dollars needed to bridge the Golden Gate Strait.

This statue of Joseph Strauss was moved in 1955 to a location that would allow people to take pictures of the bridge together with a likeness of its builder.

Hanging Around

Strauss was just five feet tall, but he was in charge of building his biggest bridge ever. On a suspension bridge such as the Golden Gate Bridge, **cables** (KAY-bulz) attached to towers hold the center sections of the bridge in place. At 4,200 feet, the Golden Gate Bridge was going to be the longest suspension bridge in the world. That was until 1964, when New York City's Verrazano Narrows Bridge opened. But at 746 feet, the Golden Gate Bridge's two towers are still the tallest in the world.

On a suspension bridge, the sections of road are held up by cables. ▶

The Great Depression

The plan to build the Golden Gate Bridge came at the right time. The United States was in the middle of the **Great Depression** (GRAYT dee-PRESH-un). The **economy** (ee-KON-uh-mee) had collapsed, thousands of businesses had failed, and one out of four people was out of work. To create jobs, cities and states all over the country developed programs to build such things as highways and bridges. The Golden Gate Bridge provided work for the people in the San Francisco area.

◀ The Golden Gate Bridge was part of a plan to create jobs for those who were out of work because of the Depression.

The Building Begins

Construction on the bridge began in February 1933 and lasted for four years. More than 200,000 people went to the ceremony celebrating the start of this construction.

Bridge workers wore hard hats and safety ropes around their waists to protect them from falling. A safety net was strung below the bridge. It was one of the safest building jobs ever. Then, on February 17, 1937, some **scaffolding** (SKAF-ul-ding) holding workers broke through the safety net. Ten men died.

The workers began by building the ▶ towers to support the cables.

Golden Gate Style

Strauss came up with the design for the bridge. But husband-and-wife **architects** (AR-kih-tekts) Irving and Gertrude Morrow gave the bridge its sleek, **art deco** (ART DEK-oh) style. The towers were carved to let the sunshine sparkle off them. The walkway railings were spread out and made thinner so that people driving across the bridge could see the view. And the window-like openings in the towers get smaller near the top. This makes the towers look even taller than they are!

◀ Engineers and architects worked together to create the beautiful Golden Gate Bridge.

A Colorful Bridge

When the bridge was built, the U.S. Navy wanted it to be painted with black and yellow stripes. They thought those colors would be easy for passing ships to see. But Irving Morrow had decided to have the bridge painted a special shade of orange, a color called **vermillion** (ver-MIL-yun). Morrow thought that the color blended well with the color of the nearby hills. Some people worried that the whole bridge would need to be painted each year. But the first paint job lasted for 27 years!

Architect Irving Morrow thought that the orange-brown color of vermillion would fit well with the hills near the bridge. ▶

Finished at Last

The Golden Gate Bridge was finished on May 26, 1937. The next day, it was opened to **pedestrians** (peh-DES-tree-enz). During the first twelve hours that the bridge was open, nearly 300,000 people paid five cents each to walk across it. On May 28, the bridge was opened to cars. That day, 32,300 cars crossed the bridge. A **toll** (TOHL) of 50 cents was charged for each car, its driver, and up to three **passengers** (PAS-en-jerz). Extra passengers had to pay five cents each. The money earned from tolls helps pay for improvements on and repairs to the bridge.

◀ Engineers and others are working to make sure that the Golden Gate Bridge lasts well into the future.

Happy Birthday, Bridge!

Few 50th birthday parties have been as big as the one celebrated on Sunday, May 24, 1987. The Golden Gate party began with "Bridgewalk '87." More than 300,000 people from around the world walked across the famous bridge. Some of these people had also walked across the bridge when it first opened in 1937. A parade of **antique** (an-TEEK) cars, some older than the bridge, followed the people. In celebration of the big day, no one had to pay a toll that day.

The Golden Gate Bridge was built to last. Today, engineers are working hard to make sure that it will do just that.

Glossary

antique (an-TEEK) Something made a long time ago.

architect (AR-kih-tekt) A person who designs and oversees the building of structures.

art deco (ART DEK-oh) A style of design, using bold outlines and many shapes.

cable (KAY-bul) Strong, thick bundles of wires.

design (dee-ZYN) The plan and look of how something is built.

engineer (en-jin-EER) A person who designs and builds things.

economy (ee-KON-uh-mee) The way a country manages its money.

Great Depression (GRAYT dee-PRESH-un) A period of time that lasted from 1929 to 1939 during which the economy in the United States collapsed, and when many people were out of work.

passenger (PAS-en-jer) A traveler in an aircraft, bus, ship, train, or car.

pedestrian (peh-DES-tree-en) Someone who is walking somewhere.

scaffolding (SKAF-ul-ding) A high platform that workers can stand on.

strait (STRAYT) A narrow channel of water that connects two larger bodies of water.

suspension (sus-PEN-shun) When something, such as a bridge platform, is hung by cables.

toll (TOHL) A fee paid for something, such as the right to cross a bridge.

vermillion (ver-MIL-yun) A bright orange-brown color.

Index